WINGED WITNESSES

African
POETRY
BOOK SERIES

Series editor: Kwame Dawes

WINGED WITNESSES

Chisom Okafor

University of Nebraska Press | Lincoln

Acknowledgments for the use of copyrighted
material appear on pages ix–x, which constitute
an extension of the copyright page.

The University of Nebraska Press is part of a land-
grant institution with campuses and programs
on the past, present, and future homelands of
the Pawnee, Ponca, Otoe-Missouria, Omaha,
Dakota, Lakota, Kaw, Cheyenne, and Arapaho
Peoples, as well as those of the relocated Ho-
Chunk, Sac and Fox, and Iowa Peoples.

The African Poetry Book Series is operated by
the African Poetry Book Fund. The APBF was
established in 2012 with initial support from
philanthropists Laura and Robert F. X. Sillerman.
The founding director of the African Poetry Book
Fund is Kwame Dawes, Holmes University Professor
and Glenna Luschei Editor of *Prairie Schooner*.

For customers in the EU with safety/
GPSR concerns, contact:
gpsr@mare-nostrum.co.uk
Mare Nostrum Group BV
Mauritskade 21D
1091 GC Amsterdam
The Netherlands

Library of Congress
Cataloging-in-Publication Data
Names: Okafor, Chisom,
1993– author
Title: Winged witnesses
/ Chisom Okafor.
Description: Lincoln: University
of Nebraska Press, 2025. | Series:
African poetry book series
Identifiers: LCCN 2025015462
ISBN 9781496243423 paperback
ISBN 9781496245885 epub
ISBN 9781496245892 pdf
Subjects: BISAC: POETRY /
African | LCGFT: Poetry
Classification: LCC
PR9387.9.O37473 W56
2025 | DDC 821.915—dc23/
eng/20250514
LC record available at https://
lccn.loc.gov/2025015462

Set in Garamond Premier
Pro by A. Shahan.

Designed by N. Putens.

For my father, Jonas.

For Onyekwelu, Sochima, and Chidera.

And for Hamna Labeeb, teacher and comrade.

CONTENTS

ACKNOWLEDGMENTS

Thanks to Kwame Dawes, Emily Wittman, D. M. Aderibigbe, Gbenga Adesina, Rachael Boast, Sarah Ladipo Manyika, and Tryphena Yeboah for all the support and mentorship.

I'm also grateful to Joel Brouwer, Wendy Rawlings, John Estes, Kwoya Maples, Taylor Brorby, and the amazing faculty at the University of Alabama's Creative Writing MFA program.

Thanks to the tribe at Oklahoma, who continue to support my work: Aunt Cecilia, Aunt Irene, Thomas, Andrea, Brandon, Ansel, and Randy.

Thanks to colleagues from the Writers' Community of the University of Nigeria, Nsukka, for that first push: Osinachi, Michael Umoh, JK Anowe, Muna, Pius, Arinze Ifeakandu, Otosirieze Obi-Young, and Ebenezer Agu.

I'm immensely grateful to these wonderful writers and contemporaries, most of whom have read and workshopped some of the poems in this book: Iquo (Oboe), Abdulkareem, Charis, Chinua, Lydia, Ramon, Laura, Will, and Maggie.

Finally, to all African poets who continue to contribute in many different ways to ongoing conversations around chronic illness and familial relationships, thank you all very much!

I am also grateful to the editors of the following journals and magazines, in which versions of these poems have appeared or are forthcoming:

The Account: "There Are No Synonyms for *Catharsis*"

Beloit Poetry Journal: "In Telephone Conversation with My Father Where He Enquires about My Marriage Plans"

Brittle Paper: "In the Palms of Night"

FIYAH: "Telepathy"

The Hellebore: "Synonyms for *Tachycardia*"

Isele: "Echo-cardio-gram," "In Another Life, I Am Twenty-Two, Gifted and Curious," and "Woodsmoke"

Jacar One: "Hymn to the Bowstring"

Jalada: "I Reach Out for My Epiphany as though I Were a River Boy Rowing Softly into the Sunset" and "Lamb of God"

Lolwe: "Throat Song"

A Long House: "As Heraclitus Steps into Five Cowries Creek the Second Time," "Birdhouse," "Old Coffee Shop," and "Teach Me to Shape-Shift"

North Dakota Quarterly: "All I Know about an Enlarged Heart Is How to Carry It"

Nigerian NewsDirect (Poetry Column): "Cachexia"

Olongo Magazine: "Some Places Become Homes by Habit"

Palette Poetry: "Child of the Sea"

Prairie Schooner: "Note to Departure," "Supersedure," and "Unlearning the Principles of Displacement for a Body at Rest"

Rattle: "Birthing"

The Raven Review: "Circumnavigation"

Yaba Left Review: "Otherwise, I Choose to Die Intestate" and "A Piercing through the Dark"

WINGED WITNESSES

FIRST WITNESS

You can only unwrap a child once.
The rest is prayer and even more prayer.
—Chris Abani, "Incantation"

Cachexia

In response to Billy Collins's "The First Night."

I am holding on to the past like a monochrome photograph
to my chest, listening to your heart
beat against mine in this untouched dark.
You say something about the past
not holding water anymore,
a forecast of hands, yours held against the darkness.

Let them go, you say.
*The secret to understanding Einstein's thoughts on relativity
is not far away from us*, you say.

There is an orchard of hearts where ours orbit each other
against the giant star of death,
and are helmed in by a curvature in space-time,
never falling completely into it
but never drifting away, too,
in an ever-evolving ring of grief.

You read me Jiménez in the fading light
straining with each stroke of dusk to catch the printed words
above the insurgent cataracts, already overtaking
the city of your eyes.
The hardest thing about death must be the first night,
you read.

And Billy Collins:
you have me wondering
if there will also be a sun and a moon
and will the dead gather to watch them rise and set.

In a parallel universe, when we've tired the sun
with our talking
and having sent her down the sky,
I see you walk to the gramophone to play my favorite record,
a gift of dirges from a father to his departing son.
You invite me to a dance
but my limbs, cachectic tonight, collapse just
before our ritual begins.

Some Places Become Homes by Habit

> *When the thousands*
> *of mysterious Sumerian tablets were translated,*
> *they seemed to be business records. But what if they*
> *are poems or psalms? My joy is the same as twelve*
> *Ethiopian goats standing silent in the morning light.*
> . . . .
> *Shiploads of thuya are what*
> *my body wants to say to your body.*
> —JACK GILBERT, "The Forgotten Dialect of the Heart"

I know, by science, the exact time it takes to row from one end of this river
to the other end, near the distant islands of São Tomé.

I know, provided the energy exerted between two strokes of the paddle
remains constant, what it takes to sail across vast swathes of water,
    unmarked

except by seals of light from the dying sun. One day, bathed in sun-spill and
a shade of orange like the yolk of an egg, I rowed with my lover to a place

where none but the river hawks could find us—as they journeyed home
    in a formation
after the day's labor—here you could see the pebbles, brown

and slippery, nestled closely underneath the clear body of water. Here, we
    stopped
to wait for deep into nightfall, when we'd let ourselves be struck by the gold

plummet of the moon, while the reverberations overpowered us in a
     nocturnal symphony
and the damp smell of decaying timber rose like a thousand voices

from the body of our fisherman's boat. My lover threw little stones into
     the river
to see the ripples spread apart and dissolve within a circumference

then in between strokes of the paddle. I heard them whisper to the
     evening air:
in this place of waters, every man is a gambler, throwing random dice

with his own life as wager, after which they disappeared through a trapdoor
and would never be seen again. But tonight, as I look up to the full moon

in its bright elegance, it seems as though my lover is back to lean again,
     against
the hairy chambers of my chest, drawing imaginary vignettes with the tips
     of their fingers,

as we let the canoe navigate itself away from questioning eyes, as again,
     we return home
to a familiar smell, but also to a new aching and begin again,

the simple rites of floatation.

In Another Life, I Am Twenty-Two, Gifted and Curious

and dreaming of fleeing the world, while perched on the transom
of a stallion of the sea, breathing stale evening air off the waterline
and an entanglement of sodium chloride and ancient sea-wood.
The boy on the other side is waiting, arms outstretched
as though to receive a prodigal advancing
to the interlocking welcome of an embrace.
Worn with the fatigue of the sea, I have become skilled in the art
of smearing my sternum with white and green watermarks
and this is the year of my first diagnosis, and I'm pressing
a miniature paintbrush to my chest, tracing the shape of a heart
feeble with cardiomegaly, and whispering
the words of the scriptures back into it:
Talitha cume. Talitha cume. Feeble boy, rise up. Rise up.
And I'm thinking of what happens to the heart when its vessel—
    an entire body
—is immersed in a body of water
and left to slouch against the rippling music of immersion.
I am thinking of the calculus of bodies,
the time between Point X and Point Y—
time between immersion and bottom of the sea—the exquisite
    mathematics of drowning.

Echo-cardio-gram

Cut your heart open, you say. And I open:
Who says the dead are farther away from us

than the distance between my failing heart and yours, which I count
as nothing, even now, as we soak up the noonday sun. Who says there are no

murmurs grinding away beneath me, when a miracle of hands, pressed on
my chest
leave me gasping for a last violence of air in sunlight. Take air as vehicle,
or fuel

for naked light, as it travels in a free fall through a vacuum, half expecting
to be caught.
Do you know what it means to fall and not be caught till a shattering arrives
to offer some relief?

Like an agony of lights from a thousand distant stars: cell phone–holding
species
whose illuminations, shed a million years back, but without the mercy

of being caught midway, are just reaching us tonight.

But there are no absolutes, you say, *and time, like truth, is relative,*
which is also to say nothing of the benevolence of the earth that stops
all free falls.

Earth, to which all travelers must return, when the day is spent

and the dance is over, and I see all the people I ever loved rise before me
like vapor from chamomile tea. And I see all the cities I ever fled from
   return to reclaim

from the barren fields souls which were theirs before time began.
   These days,
I philosophize more on death than the last man caught in the volcanic
   rage of Pompeii

with his daughter, a mass of solidified ash freshly preserved in his arm,
   as though
he was saying to the fire: *Let her body only be taken by the things she*
   never saw.

For the things you possess the least knowledge of don't really kill you.
Hear me out: On my first trip to the cardiologist's,

a man had stared at me in the waiting room
as though he was a teacher who had scribbled questions on a rough
   cardboard surface,

What caused your heart dysfunction, son?
Was it an excess of nicotine or the freedom of alcohol or both?

But I know nothing of these things. Just as an owl dies, knowing nothing
   of the etiology
of its nocturnal fondness, why only in empty darkness is where it
   finds home.

But we misinterpret emptiness as guilt,
which is why the owl is a curious creature to us.

See how easy it is to confuse falling with the act of falling?

See how we swiftly tend to fall into the things that fail us
like the reverberations of this cardiac machine, faithful in its representation

of how much closer I am to the end of my heart dysfunction
than I think.

Animalcules

What first greets anyone who enters this room
is not the medication, not my drooping eyes,
tarrying undecided between recovery and relapse,
but the old bible left on the stool, just beside my bed
where my father's hand can swiftly reach it.
At midnight, he flips it open and for a long while
stares at the vignette of the Last Supper
on the first page, as if to crawl inside it
and save Jesus from imminent death
then I hear him recite his favorite bible verse
into his palms, supple with anointing oil,
his mouth dense with the book of Isaiah:
Ma ndi n'ele anya Chineke . . . ga-agbanwe ike ha
Ha ga-agba óso, ike agaghi agwukwa ha
Ha ga-eje ije, ghara ida mba.

But those who wait for God . . . will renew their strength
They will run, and not be weary
They will walk, and not faint.

Afterward, he keeps vigil, his breaths
steady and drawn against the long moan
of the night like a snake's hiss. His head
is bowed in a catnap, the way St. Francis
must have appeared on the night
of his first missionary trip, bent with exhaustion.
I fall into a trance and there is an army of bacteria
invading my body's defenses
dressed in deceitful clothing.

They populate the islets of Langerhans
slice through the sphincter of Oddi
infiltrate the Bowman's capsule
graze on the walls of the Cowper's gland
and curl round the loop of Henle
while I'm left muttering every one of god's names
I ever committed to memory
Rapha. Jaireh. Sabaoth
which is my most preferred name for god
Sabaoth: a platoon of insurgents
charioting into my body,
an invasion of an already-invaded land.
But it's hard to think about horses when
my father's voice stubbornly tickles my ears
and his prayers keep falling like many
little animals on my infected chest
as I pretend to fall asleep.

Teach Me to Shape-Shift

We sit at the point where Carter Bridge
begins to gain some ascendancy,
and I follow the trajectory of your left finger,
pointing away to the moon, its pearly robe
of silver, nothing tonight but heraldic.

I let my line of sight dribble into the shoreline beyond,
it stops at the point where a girl performs her laundry
in the palm of night
and spits lather into the mouth of the sea.
In this way, she lends liquefied portions
of her body to the deep histories of floatation.

Behind her, her brother, still a toddler
negotiates the boundary between sea and earth
tending to a sand house
like a woman beautifying a bride before her wedding.
His twinkling eyes seem for a moment
to consider the technicalities of structuring
in clay, translating Fahrenheit to Celsius, ounces
to pounds, stones to kilograms, in the untouched dark.

My eyes linger so long as not to distinguish anymore
the points of convergence
between twilight and full nightfall.
So long, they linger at the hinges of childhood and youth.

Not even the best music of the sea can save the eyes of my heart
from this journey into memory.
Not even the sea itself, boisterous with history
nor the resplendence of speedboats tied to the jetty
and motionless tonight.

Supersedure

At nightfall, as always, I meet him
just at the foot of Carter Bridge, brown skin

catching the receding sun. His eyes rush out to meet mine in the soft light

just before they wander off again, far
into this body of water, as if to drag the eye of the waves into the sunset
    and beyond.

In his head is the door of a deserted house
left unlatched, a window open to the sea upon which are stranded canoes.

He searches for answers to a prayer long lost to the winds
and the water below running marathons, seeking to break free of the surface.

Even journeying is a form of prayer. Perhaps this wayfarer has come a long way

shedding layers of skin already heavy with the fatigue
of fleeing. This tongue, hidden in a body that knows the weight

of many morning years is now, in its evening years, burdened
by its own shadow. This twisted mouth has known love like a salmon knows

the damp air of rivers, of another man waiting for a son who left
and never returned. How long do we have until the things we love start
    to kill us?

Circumnavigation

You suggest we journey into the daybreak
with tales of war; how the warriors of the East
by doing the unimaginable to themselves
did more to others, violence making things whole again.
In my head, a flower has just begun
to sprout, headed for a miracle of sunshine.
I imagine there is a fleeing antelope arriving from my chest,
thinking of the complicated act of escape
and kicking
this hibiscus, in all of its youthful allure
to the possibility of an early death
even in the face of an abundance of photosynthesis.
Applause of spring or joy
of bloom.
How a half-life
even for the youngest of hibiscuses,
is wholeness in itself

On Your Second Visit to the Cardiologist

Your eyes are trained on the peaks and valleys
of the electrocardiograph, forging infinitely ahead.
Your thought strays, distorted, against the hum
of cardiac machines.
Distortion is a twisting out of shape, like a cavalry of ants
struck by an insurrection within their own ranks.

Distortion is an artificial translation given
to the body's catabolic responses,
the muscles of the heart constantly undergoing
a biology of breakdown
and yours being a winged witness to this phenomenon.
How long before you begin your long walk home?
The doctor's assistant asks
if you've ever fallen into something heavier than darkness.
Like a coma.
For you, it's this room of cardiac machines. These plugs.
This beeping tragedy.

You know the English synonyms for *apocalypse*
as fists of cumulonimbus gathering overhead.
Yet, this is not a narrative about clouds or failing organs
for to believe in the failing of things is to become yourself, something
worse than the signaling of an end.

You're still etherized on the examination table
while the cardiologist palpates your chest, dips his stethoscope into flesh,
orders you to inhale some antiseptic air.

I need you to hold your breath for three secs.
Now, exhale. Good.
You keep counting the hours.
How much longer before you begin your long walk home?

All I Know about an Enlarged
Heart Is How to Carry It

Again, I wake to an entangling—
pallor announcing itself by the purple patches on my palms

my head swirling with the ambience of pebbles
thrown down the cliff of a hill.

I carry my heart so well that even death, encircling overhead
cannot breach its defenses.

When my lover says: how are you today?
their voice rings out from the doorway

and leaves heart-shaped imprints on the wall, like a percussion
of stranded pigeons

calling for help in a deserted alleyway.
Their voice is like their fear. It gives them away.

Their face is aglow with thanks
for my survival through another night

of crucifixion. But all I know
about an enlarged heart is the angina pains

that linger through nightfall and
far into the morning after.

Petrichor

You invite me to the slow violence of your body.
I could feel your delight, like rain
turbaned around the circumference
of a rain-bathing child's head,

and just after the entrance
I make a detour, convulsing
with hunger for the things
I have lost from my previous life.
Within the waves of your body
and up to the points where
the spiraling light is first refracted
before it turns impenetrable
like a passage through
a prism of glass
opaque and translucent in equal measure,

I search for a song
that used to be mine
but which has now become a sailor's talisman lost at sea
and believed to be nestled
between membranes and tissues of your body.

There is a story hidden within the story
of my departure from home.
Peep through, and you'll see my father
clutching a chest already squeezed out
with angina pains, or an uncle

dying slowly from an affliction
that has refused to grow old.

It is hard to die, he says to me.
It is life we should be afraid of, not death.

Lay me on the shelter of this new knowingness.
Sing me a buffet of vocables,
an à la carte of phosphenes until I'm satiated.

It's seven years after my drifting
apart, but I still fail at the subtle art
of forging recovery psalms.
Tell me, how do you forgive what has refused
to stop punishing you?
How do you return to the sweet agonies of a previous life?

Thunderhead

Here, where the light from the moon mushrooms
over the city and cocoons around you
transfiguring into a liquid film
and dripping from your face
to which you seem oblivious,
I watch you count between the tips of your fingers
the English alphabets for the Japanese word
given to the art of mending fabric:

sashiko

Little stabs, you say in translation.
There, at the heart of mending
is the resplendent art of destruction.
The night cloud, starless in its docility
is a nocturnal cumulonimbus, dressed in deceitful garments.
I know the songs your throat longs to sing
tonight
before the moon disappears
and the brewing turbulence returns.
But even knowing is an illusion when raised
against this litmus blanketing
of nightfall.

There Are No Synonyms for *Catharsis*

on the thesaurus of hearts.
Only fear, then nothing
situated in between.
You wonder what the moon in all of its opaque
resplendence
would become tonight
without a beholder and with its lights of silver
left hemorrhaging
into this empty room while we drown ourselves
within a lullaby.
You suddenly stop to ask
if my joy, long lost, has returned,

but I respond in the way of being curious in my unhappiness
and curious in my joys
and in my silence there is a force
acting to cause a displacement
within my body,

a force equal and opposite
to the powerhouse of my body.
What does it mean to be a fruit
tarrying, undecided
between ripening and decay?

Even a vain thing as indecision
possesses the power to change
every man.

Tonight, I come to you, a man in the face of his epiphany.
Dear lover, watch me sift into the heart of the night,
watch me echolocate,
watch me trip over a rock just as I prep
my heart for disaster,
each of the human eye being god's loneliest creation
and hidden away
each in its socket,
each without knowledge of the presence of an "other"
a few inches across the street
of the nose,

and my body, synonym for *utopia*
rising from the Greek word
utopus, which is to say *best place,*

but which also means *no place, waterless*
if you defer to its original translation.

Tonight, I listen to my heart
whisper double-faced promises
in my hearing:
I'll take you out, it says,
which is to say *dine with you,*
which is also to say
suffocate you.

Woodsmoke

Falling, by which I mean a synchronized
art of dying. By which I also mean something
burning in my chest

as I skid at full velocity off the middle
of a rail track.
I want to say to a century

of twinkling species overhead:
I, too, have been touched by wildfire
in a previous life
I, too, have memorized the simple art
of free-falling.

On Breaking the News of My Heart Dysfunction, I Knew We Would Never Be the Same

That night, the wind, when it arrived
as an orchestra of throbbing air

blowing up plumes of dust from the mountains overhead,
blew up, too, tufts of your hair

as though to gift them to the fields—
a memento in forgetfulness.
But here, within this orchard of hearts, is buried
all the memories we can ever make,

buried in clay but also alive. I long to kneel before you
as in a trance, to make a stockpile of confessions,
leave them trailing after me, in the brief moment
that would precede my departure.

Which is to say, I'm drinking up
my joy in tots of silverware with their trademark lacquer
long lost to the inevitable physics
of time and decay.

But in describing the science of my dying,
I make a vignette of a man, forgotten in his sleep of death.

This is my most preferred posture of departure:
to fall asleep on a sofa
and forget the moment of my awakening.

angina decubitus

In the face of darkness, I'm giving names
to the days before my first myocardial infarction,

by which I mean counting off the tips of my fingers,
the intervening moments
between each clinical manifestation:

Dizziness, fatigue, lethargy,
an agonizing force rising in rebellion
from deep within my shoulder blades
to invoke breathlessness into my supine body.

Signs are the demons you see,
symptoms are what permit you the sense of feeling.

I've been a perpetual marathoner in the nocturnal
sport of insomnia, but tonight I'm deep in sleep
and dreaming of rows of peppercorn seeds
in a deserted orchard

stretching into thin lines and receding
far beyond the courageous advances of the eyes
and deep into the distance of this night.

I'm journeying alone and lost among pines
rising to whisper choruses to the moon
then falling back.

On Patmos, the Isle of My Departure

Look, how gracefully the wind caresses my face
even in the surprise

of wounded-ness.

What seems to be patience
is a kind of pain
in itself.

What becomes of the prey floating away with the kite
unguarded, save for the illuminations
of the fading,
golden-yellow sun?

I'm thinking of this unfortunate thrush
journeying with the sky-predator
to an end, taking place in the dawn of her own life.

In Light of Saint John's Testimony as Recorded in the Morning Light on the Water Lands of Patmos

And when the doctor's voice rises like carbon smoke
and diffuses round the room in layers
before receding by the doorway—its floral patterning
growing unrecognizable—
I imagine the moment of unease on a vessel when one,
having set sail, finally loses sight of land.

In the beginning, you say the sea was without form
and the last of the daylight came shafting through each open doorway
of this floating house,
falling across its rooms in orange ribbons.
And I respond by whispering:
My body is, in its weakest moments, a mesh of gulfweed
and reed and bulrush breaking free
unto the face of the sea.

You say the world has long
stopped listening to my arrhythmic heartbeats
and now vacillates in an ever-revolving
cycle of darkness,
but what I see is the light seeping through the crevices on the wall
of this desolate room
and falling all around us.

Stranglehold

They'd only done what all along they'd come
intending to do. So they lay untouched by regret,
after.
—CARL PHILLIPS, "For It Felt Like Power"

We build a pyre
and start to make a pact off the flames
here, in the middle of the world,
which doubles as the focal point of nowhere,
we trace the twinkling locomotion of glowworms,
count moments between each illumination and the next.
These nights are theirs, you tell me,
and so is the world.
We're only nocturnal guests of these species.
And at once, a secret, kept in time as a wellspring, is revealed.
And in knowing, I say: These are the lucky ones.
For, to shed all the little lights of the world
and not yourself, be bereft of light in the end
as to need daily medication, is in itself
a gift.

It's hard to take this confession as mine,
harder still to believe that I can ever say so.

As Heraclitus Steps into Five Cowries Creek the Second Time

For it is not the same river and he is not the same man

And here, I'm lost on a boat
that overlooks the city
in all of its ugliness and all of its beauty.
I desire this unending
song taking place
within this swathe of water serenading a motionless
parade of lights
and its extension to many nautical miles
more than I can ever admit,
my boat, parting the waters
ever so slightly into two frontiers
before they're covered up again
in a shadow of silver as though nothing ever
rowed passed—
for some things need to be nudged
so as to remain unchanged—and for a moment in a rising
of waves, I swear I can hear
the invitations of the deep
far beyond, and crashing
mightily into tidal sequence,
this call and response of the sea:
Take my hand. Take my hand.
Come home, come home, child of the sea.

I Gift You a Miracle of Pills

A coin for every prescribed medication:
2.5 milligrams bisoprolol fumarate
to be taken once daily,
five milligrams amlodipine besilate
to be taken once daily to induce blood flow,
seventy-five milligrams clopidogrel bisulphate
to be taken once, in the event of a cerebrovascular accident.
A daily dose of diuretics
to keep your feet from surrendering
to a plague of floods.
Think of a body of water as an enlargement
or *edema* in medical terms.
Think of *oidein* as a fourteenth-century word for *edema*,
which means to swell, to rise
or to give rise
to another life through a miracle
of arteries dying every day and
rising to life again
and again.

Synonyms for *Tachycardia*

Synonyms for *tachycardia* are pebbles flung
into the night,
are a shower of leaves
falling off their branches on a day full of wind.
In my aloneness, I pull two bread slices into a magnetic field
with avocado for butter.
I make a vegetable sandwich out of the void
like a god
on his creation morning. I want to pretend
I'm not at the edge of ruin.
I want to look toward the rising sun
and say to it:
Do not feel sorry for me, for what is empathy
if not a further annihilation of an already dead thing.
Once in a telephone conversation,
my father lowered his voice and asked:
have you had lunch, son?
by which he actually meant:
have you fallen sick again?
Have you lost your appetite?
Are you nauseous?
Are you lethargic?

Night

Not even the smell of burnt-out cigarettes
lingering in the air, long after their owners have departed

into that starry night; not even the night itself
or the road that winds into its palm

could dissuade the hunger from rising
from within my eyes, here, in the cold shivers of a wintry sunset.

You reach for a swig of grey goose vodka and
I see your hands, outstretched into the approaching dark, a toast to our

newfound companionship, but I do not tell you
how almost impossible it is to reclaim the things long lost to youth

and you do not see the silence chewing away at me.
Gnawing and gnawing.

Birdhouse

I do not keep diaries to save myself anymore
or the people I love,
or love itself.
Here in the first light of August, a songbird rests on an almond branch,
and soft with gratitude for the arrival of light,
bursts into psalms.

From a gyrating branch, I watch lovers as they make their triumphant entry—
honey seekers in a deserted apiary—
then I see them depart in a hurry, like all others before them,
and like the ones who had come before the ones who had come before them
not wanting to carry my overbearing deadweight;
not wanting to be scarred for the rest of their lives.

Before now, I used to think death was
the nothing every other thing returns to
but it's safer, I suppose, to learn by practice, to shut out the sun
from my eyes, and become a hand, cupped
over the ears of the hundredth lover, whispering:

I must warn you, dear august guest
that my heart is a nest sashaying in the wind.
A literal heart, I mean. And a metaphoric nest. I must warn you.
For, in all my life, I have been human only nine times.
Then, at the end of my ninth cardiac session, I paddled away
and my canoe has not been sighted ever since.

Soul brother.

Disregard what you see from your window in the noonday sun.
This house is falling. Swinging like the fulcrum of a door
left ajar, on a day full of wind.
In an orchard of hearts, mine is a pear tree, overridden with spikes.

Hunger, Even in the Face of a Foreshadowing

And you teach me to pray in this way, and in this way, you teach me
the path of being led into terror.
—Kwame Dawes, "How I Pray in the Plague"

My body bears a history of storms
bruising the trees, in an expanse populated with cactuses.
My suffering greater than my lover's,
displaces theirs, as in when the echo of my voice
fills the perimeters of a room
and my body is the heaviest luggage in the closet.

I imagine sailing to the array of lights scattered at a harbor
and dancing when viewed from the translucent waters
at sundown
when my body is a conglomeration of trees
bursting into a prophesy full of colors
of a surrendering to gunpowder and to a fusillade of lead.

Consider that the heart's place in the chest has been used for ages
as a point of target in any firing squad,
for the heart is more prominent and is, as a result,
an easier target than the forehead.

Which is to say, when I finally
kneel to pray for respite from this uprising
taking place in my cardiac regions, it's so I can set free, what waits
    to detonate
from within me.

It's so I can stream through widening channels into an open sea
knowing my heart to be a drowning place for men:
a place of epiphany,
a place of prophesy,
but also an endpoint, unto itself.

I Reach Out for My Epiphany as though I Were a River Boy Rowing Softly into the Sunset

On evenings like this, I choose boyhood again
to feel the soft chorus of water
and the makeshift jetty, dug deep
into the bottom of the river, in its silvery elegance.

I know how softly, too, my body travels
with this water, how it advances
in diagonal lines of waves
how it disappears as the waves crash against my canoe
and I let myself slip
underneath my own skin, to safety.

On an expedition, my lover whispered
from the hard deck of their own canoe
out in the evening cold:
trust everyone. But trust no one.
Which is to say, never feel sorry for this skin
which you now call home.
Or the love you choose to feed it,
or the life you choose to gift it.

And I knew at once, to approach this body the way a butcher
comes to the slaughter with hunger to kill, so as to save
a household when the day is spent.

So, I long for nightfall by the sea;
a preamble to a story I'd soon be able to tell,
to give thanks for the things my body has finally become:

a child again.
Benign again.
To feed me a serving of relief
like seafood spat out unto dry land
washed clean again.

OTHER WITNESSES

I swim the field—stitches
everywhere, your body everywhere, blue cornflowers.
—CARL PHILLIPS, "Since You Ask"

Old Coffee Shop

You saunter into the old coffee shop
through the translucent doorway
while I follow closely, like a sinful man
who didn't need saving
but desired it anyway. At the table
we converse in hushed tones
more in the way of friends
than anything else.
You are the interpreter of my dreams
who has come to save me from the snares of the wild.

A waitress tells us of the finality of this day
for the coffee shop—
We're closing shop forever.
She barely lets out the words through teeth plastered with
an artificial smile
and a furrowed brow that has refused to stay hidden—

while *history* stares us in the face.

Beyond us, the mother of all histories bleeds.
There is conflict somewhere
distortion elsewhere
and there is blood on the windowsills
of all the firstborns in a distant country.

But suddenly, we realize *history* has already arrived at our doorsteps:
this coffee shop shutting her doors today
and us, sipping cappuccinos as memorabilia for the tongue.
This is not the land I used to know, you grieve.
This is not the land I used to know.

Like the world itself, and like me,
you say you're also in need of some transfusion
you say you're cane sugar with no sweetness left.
But I don't believe you.
If I know one person in the world who can die
for others, it is you.
If anything on this table is bitter, it must be my coffee
stripped of milk,
and if any heart in this shop needs forgiveness, it must be mine.

Note to Departure

And when, in the aftermath of our breaking apart, you
stand at the subway station, waiting to pierce,
homebound through the night
in a deserted train
the clouds above you would break into a platoon of owls
just before the dark detour of the tunnel ahead.

You should know at that moment that I, too, am a prodigal of the night,
that I see us, as in earlier times
cocooned within the fluid warmth of a blanket
into the tender light of morning.

So, I know you'll return to offer a serving of yourself again
to this starving flesh
when you become unable to bear
the sultry air of longing and its distances.

At times, I wish I could meet in a duel
the mother of *all* departures, dressed in deceitful clothes
and say: *I serve you vengeance for all the times you expelled me
into a narrow country.*

In the Palms of Night

for the stars are
luminous
phones
in the palms of night
—ROLLI, "Let Us Not Even Dream"

I have longed for this golden twinkling at sundown:
this architecture of clouds, dyed with yellow slices of light.
Tonight, a random trespasser has set fire to the hills
and two dozen weaverbirds, feather-locked,
come circumventing downhill to safety.
I could pick out the lyrics of their birdsong,
which is theirs but which also is mine.
I could engage with this familiar chirping away,
this chronicle of common loss.

I can sense the advancing wind before the night is far spent,
displaced, too, by the tidal sequences of the sea,
as it blows up plumes of debris from the dead fires
buried with the hills beyond, and more thrushes,
survivors of the night in this journey of endless distances.
I can sense the strong cologne of an imaginary lover
soft-eyed, gazing with me into the distant nights.
I tell you, there are few things more profound
than the algorithms of twin heartbeats in a city of stars
ready to meet this pure thirst for warmth in the ringing cold,
a hymn our throats yearn to sing:
Here we are, lost in your palms, night. Lost in the palms of night.
Lost in the palms of night.

Unlearning the Principles of Displacement for a Body at Rest

I'm only a boy on the night my father returns
from his former life—a country that offered him death
for two bottles of cheap wine—
hair the color of wet moss
and stranded between columns of woodsmoke
and evening air, a prayer book for exorcisms flipped open in his head.
He wades his way to shore, skin bleached by pale sunlight.
I want to say greetings, but he offers charred teeth for smiles,
a bag of bones for gifts,
bloodstained hands in lieu of an embrace.
I hurt myself with a fishhook,
curious to discover what remains of my tactile sense.
I drill a hole into the point where the tip
of my thumb should be.
I'm a scavenger, digging for diamonds in a deserted coal mine.
My father does not gather strands of my falling hair in his hands,
nor does he start to ululate
in thanksgiving, for (my) survival in his absence.
His eyes are never here nor there,
wanting love, wanting home again, wanting everything.
He says: *Come home, boy. Home is an open door.*
I say: *My body is rainwater, finding home after a rainstorm.*
So, I'll stay until deep into sundown
when the stars start to fall and hit my feet
in sparkles.
I'll stay until I no longer see his face,
heavy with liquor, nor feel the painful evidence
of his whip on my lower back.

Until I become unable to decipher sounds
nor answer to this river each time she calls:
tender notes rising, then dissolving into echoes, soft and thrumming
like sapphire tossed into her body, slicing out a neat arc in air
before sinking and causing ripples in concentric circles.
I'll stay all night until I'm washed clean again
by the dews at first light.

Jaded Feet

On my departure,
I kneel before my aging father
for blessings
but he bursts into a song instead.

There is a scent
of cut grass from the backyard
sprayed with pesticides
rising with the wind
and choking.

Choking.

The reverberation of his voice
invades my hearing
like discordant tunes
and stings like lime.

But he doesn't see the proximity
of my dying
or pretends not to see.

Otherwise, I Choose to Die Intestate

Nine times I've found myself sprawled out,
etherized on the ECG table, in a room peopled by cardiac monitors
and bespectacled cardiologists.
Nine times I've known the speed at which my heart beats
to exactly equate the velocity of light,
which is the same, I suppose, as the gravitational pressure
exerted on a given body in motion,
taken by the exquisite art of free-falling,
self-destructively.

One night, my father hid himself somewhere between bodies
stationed at the entrance of my room
while I agonized.

I swear, if I believed in forgiveness,
here is what I'd have said to him:
I forgive you for passing unto me your heart of stone.

A heart not capable of loving in the way the world has come to know it
and choosing, instead, time after time,
all the several darknesses that I hated once
but have now come to love
like the cologne of a passerby long lost to the wind.

A Piercing through the Dark

Circa 2021

In the face of darkness, this secluded space is a pathology
likewise to live alone in it.
My heart keeps failing in bits, as the voice from the evening news,
crisp as snowflakes, announces that twitter
has just been banned in my country.
It's close to bedtime and my lover is on their knees,
hunched over the bed on the other side
praying in a language only they understand.

Empty tonight, I remember walking with my father to the cardiologist's
six years ago, after I'd fallen for the fourth time
off the cliff of a hill
my feet devoid of sensations, my head swirling
as in a circumventing tornado.
When the doctor asked me to describe the pain in my chest,
I think I said *angina.*
I think I said *pectoris.*
I think I said *there is an elephant on my chest.*
I can't remember which now.
But I'm sure he heard, *My heart is clean and white as silk.*
And muttered in reply, *I know. I know.*

After praying, my lover feels God has listened too much
to my arrhythmic heartbeats.
God sees your racing heart,
Why not tell him something he has never seen?

We proceed to talk to God again about twitter and start with:
A country, velvety red. Blood red.
Red of the marooned. Red of the shipwrecked.
Red of oxygenated blood
stuck within the perimeters of an endangered heart.

There is a trembling in our bodies
precipitated by the unknown.
We can't find more words for God than these.
This is where language begins. This is where language ends.

Medical Histories

Brother, you've been here before
where a medical history form asks,
have you ever been diagnosed with a chronic disease?
I sat beside you at that moment—
in a common companionship of loss.

You've felt it before, this particular
kind of embarrassment
rising inside you like dragon-smoke,
this customary shuffle, like when you burst
into the drugstore after a long walk.
You know what it means to be known by your pharmacist
who sees you only through the lens of your illness.

On the day of your first diagnosis
you laughed and swore to never again
take the world too seriously.
There is no right and there is no wrong, you said
just the heart, where there is an angel that kills
if you do not follow it.
But I saw you holding something in your hands
which seemed like a bird-of-the-night cooing out for help.
This bird was evil and good in equal measure
the way our childhood game of stone-throwing
used to be a good omen until your stone shattered a windshield

the way the Arabic word for *passion*
can be the same for *tornado*, so that you have something
plummeting from the sky
when you think you have love

the way our father would describe
a lake in the middle of the world to put us to sleep
on nights when there was no electricity in the house
and you needed some ventilation.
The way this was the greatest truth he ever told us
and also the greatest lie.

Memories Are Traitors, They Blurt Out Time

so deftly, that we're left undecided
as if the people we ever loved, ever stared at with longing,
once existed only in a fold in time.

In a dream, my grandmother is dying
from a genetic heart condition,
but she drags her preferred bible passage with her.

I go to prepare a place for you, she recites
so that where I am, there you may also be.

I wake before I get a chance to tell her about the spasms of pain
arrowing down my left arm.

But she has become my internal rhythm
of resistance
in this city of bones.

You'll cross the barren lands and not die,
she prophesies.
You'll journey to distant lands, and not get lost
on your way home.

Child of the Sea

My father knows me by names that are not mine. Tonight, I'm the fishwife.
It doesn't really count that I share this lineage with women of the streets
or that I hear echoes of my own voice rush through his blood like a whip,
marking rivers across the back of my neck or that his fingers are piercing
when they meet my tongue to deposit scales.
This is the hidden point on a running line where two angles seem to meet
but his hand on my shoulder is a dream I don't want to escape with.
So, I wait for daybreak, more than barmen on the nightshift
wait for first signs of light.
Even more than the tigress waits for trespassers after demarcating her territory
with her urine. But far into this dark,
my father, again, calls me by another name: *You're a child of the sea.*
Invites me to take a sip of his screwdriver cocktail.
Here, sick boy, something to soften your haunted feet:
two citrus slices, angostura, tots of campari
till morning comes. Drink, river boy.
Still, I find no pleasure in sharing his drink.
Here is a testament to how much I've nurtured
the tornado in my mouth. Unforgiving. Unyielding.
In his eyes are stories, begging to be forgotten, yet always retold.

Birthing

i

Here, seven nautical miles away
we let our canoe trail the direction of wind.
Here, where all things take their roots
from this body of water; the crashing of waves
like colors strewn on palettes,
the fishing lines and their miracle of sounds
breaking through her glassy shimmer.
Here, we become pilgrims advancing by sight.

ii

When my companion casts their net
I see the hands of a javelin thrower and I want
those hands in exchange for mine,
to hold mine on nights when stars adorn the sky.
But there is no starlit constellation overhead now,
not even deep into nightfall yet
and we're rowing to the shacks on the other side
lined up on dry land in a solemn procession,
and we're pitched on both ends of this canoe, paddling away
past boat parts in disuse, past tired, retreating fishermen
past floating fish traps to dry land
where bamboo pillars find their footing
ready for the call of birds
on the riverbank.

iii

My lover swears they could trace the scape of the highlands
far into the village beyond, from this distance
the ridges stretching so thin that they disappear into the sunset.
There is a serenity in water that builds nests in my head
and shatters only when my lover grips the paddle again
for one more stroke like the swing of a broken racket
before we let us drift downstream with the tide.

iv

Consider that all waters spring from an unseen circuit.
That love is like rain droplets that announce a thunderstorm.
That love is a thunderstorm.
That love smells like soil washed clean at sunrise
by liquid, ordinary as rain.
That love is sunrise
which means that our love is the petal of a freshly watered rose
blooming in the sun.
That love is a flowing stream.
That here, on this body of water is where lovers
find their names again.

Throat Song

In this room is a body in plasters and scaffolding acting out a script.
In this script, my shape-shifting starts.

My sequined boots have known this route too well.
My hands on this windowpane are talismans for survival

which is why they bend but do not crack,
which is why I wait for an imaginary lover to emerge at nightfall

which is why I wait to spit out this song stuck in my throat ,
to burst into a symphony of rapid music as offering to their entrance

while fists of evening air drift in to paper these naked walls
dancing to their own tunes in the dark.

My mouth, a river's tributary—tells me I must rediscover redemption
in the song of a bird at the close of work, sliding into the sunset;

in the eyes of fish caught in—a net singing dirges
to a last flicker of candlelight they'll ever see;

in the peaks and valleys of an electrocardiogram
bearing terrible news. This is how you long for love at nightfall

while a wishbone grows where a lover should be.

Telepathy

At the end of short days and into longer nights,
the sun slithers home in degrees
giggling into my face.
She circles me like a badly shaped gown.
Like me, her temper is quick and sultry.
My grandfather's favorite stretcher rests,
serpentine, on the porch.
Never touch, I'm told
Never offend the dead.
But I crawl with the night to sit on its shadow.
He starts to light pipe after pipe
Gifting whirls of smoke to the sky.
His mouth twitches into a knowing smile when owls screech
in the distance.
The moon, journeying with us into the night,
bursts into an array of clouds
and for long moments
we let our weary eyes linger on her fading light.

Lamb of God

i

Here is what we're told:
The dead come alive shortly after midnight
which is why, midway, the night hardens into dogs, howling.
Tonight, I wait to see your face
in the night rain,
as water streams
through the gaps between my fingers,
zigzag lines of night rain
bursting through the wind
and again, I'm a child. Again, I'm stranded between voids.

ii

The dead do not really die,
they journey, with the silence of God's lambs
across the bridge over Jahannam
where all humans must pass,
narrow as spiderweb, slippery as catfish skin.

iii

Dear lover,
I hear your voice, narrow as a needle, in the fading light.
Soft and slippery as the rustle of leaves on nights when
the sky is a starlit constellation, and darkness
is a woman of many names.
But tonight, your face is the moon I drink while
I squeeze you out of the shadows, watch
you cringe like an out-of-season fruit,
extracting juice from itself.

iv

I am told:

A fisherman in my dream

explains my lover seeking departure from their former life.

I sneeze at noon, when they call from the other side.

I know them like I know a gmelina tree stripped clean of leafage

after a windstorm.

I'm told: *Never whistle in the dark*

you call them back from the bridge they already crossed.

v

Dead lambs of God do not really die,

they wait for new names,

Or wait for a reunion with their lovers

on the bridge over Jahannam.

There Is No Haloing Attached to These Bodies

On a sinking slave ship, a man sings a lullaby
of Igbo mythology
to his sleeping sons,
The words are shaky
but muscled together
into an abbreviation of a thing
eating up itself
within itself. Autophagic, biologically.

He invites them to come journey with him
to a swathe of land only reachable
by witnessing to the turbulence of the sea.

Mmiri mụrụ anyi.
Mmiri na-akpọ anyi.

But there is no haloing attached
to these bodies being worked up for imminent loss.

For a moment, they're deaf to the invitations of the deep;
the waves, impatient and dashing
with the violence of nine hundred men
clashing against themselves.

There is no salvation in his eyes,
no remedial psalm
lurking within the shadows
of the deep.

Shadows navigate more shadows
to meet the strange violence of hope
for a miracle to spring forth
from this finality of grief
as he sings to his sleeping sons.

The Voice that Comes with the Winds at Nightfall Is a Traveler's, Dying inside My Head

His socks,
two burning cities, rise like carbon-smoke.

The wind undressing him is best served cold
best unveiled in the space between full-light and sundown.

Beyond closed eyes, he sees the world again
a drift of bodies, an elegy to birds migrating with rainclouds in August.

The voice I hear belongs to a drowning boy,
is an undecipherable murmur of expelled rain, melting into droplets

back where they'd come from,
is a city under siege, is baobab sucked clean of leafage after a storm.

Moment after moment, I strain to catch him, the singer
on the borderline, while he carves patterns of a broken cello with clay

to gift the setting sun before he goes to sleep
facing a home whose doors may never swing open.

Hymn to the Bowstring

Given affliction, the body will find a way,
the body will turn itself
to music.
—JOSEPH FASANO, "St. Vitus' Dance"

At times I like to imagine that the rains made branches
hang more heavily, so that some swept the dust

that would soon become a burial place
for an offspring of leaves.

My lover knows the principles of death as rationale
for this floral survival phenomenon, wherein a cycle has to end

for another to commence.

Sometimes, I want to admit to feeling the weight of the world
stockpiled in my head, but they call me *hashashin*

which means bound in perpetuity to *hashish*, which means creed
which means bowstring sworn to its archer and to the holy act of
   destruction

I say, destroy this body and before daybreak, I'll raise it up,
which is to say I want this body to love in the gratifying way of
   sideways rain

that levitates with the monsoon at daybreak
and leaves flower funnels waterlogged and longing to unfurl at
   noon again

for another chance at light.

In Telephone Conversation with My Father Where He Enquires about My Marriage Plans

A dagger navigating through a gulf of wire curls
meets the center point of my forehead
just after he spells out the words

lost between the frontiers of things
I desire and what I must be.
I want to tell him about the ringing cold

or about the house sparrow who, homeless
after her tree was felled, had made
her nest just at the edge of my windowsill.

Instead, I say: Daddy, I don't think the telephone
line is clear enough for this
conversation.

Beating the Graves
Tsitsi Ella Jaji

*Keorapetse Kgositsile: Collected
Poems, 1969–2018*
Keorapetse Kgositsile
Edited and with an introduction
by Phillippa Yaa de Villiers
and Uhuru Portia Phalafala

'mamaseko
Thabile Makue

Stray
Bernard Farai Matambo
Foreword by Kwame Dawes

The Rinehart Frames
Cheswayo Mphanza
Foreword by Kwame Dawes

Origins of the Syma Species
Tares Oburumu
Foreword by Kwame Dawes

Winged Witnesses
Chisom Okafor

Gabriel Okara: Collected Poems
Gabriel Okara
Edited and with an introduction
by Brenda Marie Osbey

The Gathering of Bastards
Romeo Oriogun

Sacrament of Bodies
Romeo Oriogun

The Kitchen-Dweller's Testimony
Ladan Osman
Foreword by Kwame Dawes

Mine Mine Mine
Uhuru Portia Phalafala

Leaked Footages
Abu Bakr Sadiq
Foreword by Kwame Dawes

Mummy Eaters
Sherry Shenoda
Foreword by Kwame Dawes

Fuchsia
Mahtem Shiferraw

Your Body Is War
Mahtem Shiferraw
Foreword by Kwame Dawes

In a Language That You Know
Len Verwey

Loving the Dying
Len Verwey

When We Only Have the Earth
Abdourahman A. Waberi
Translated by Nancy
Naomi Carlson

204

Logotherapy
Mukoma Wa Ngugi

Breaking the Silence: Anthology
of Liberian Poetry
Edited by Patricia Jabbeh Wesley

When the Wanderers Come Home
Patricia Jabbeh Wesley

Seven New Generation African
Poets: A Chapbook Box Set
Edited by Kwame Dawes
and Chris Abani
(Slapering Hol)

Eight New-Generation African
Poets: A Chapbook Box Set
Edited by Kwame Dawes
and Chris Abani
(Akashic Books)

New-Generation African Poets:
A Chapbook Box Set (Tatu)
Edited by Kwame Dawes
and Chris Abani
(Akashic Books)

New-Generation African Poets:
A Chapbook Box Set (Nne)
Edited by Kwame Dawes
and Chris Abani
(Akashic Books)

New-Generation African Poets:
A Chapbook Box Set (Tano)
Edited by Kwame Dawes
and Chris Abani
(Akashic Books)

New-Generation African Poets:
A Chapbook Box Set (Sita)
Edited by Kwame Dawes
and Chris Abani
(Akashic Books)

New-Generation African Poets:
A Chapbook Box Set (Saba)
Edited by Kwame Dawes
and Chris Abani
(Akashic Books)

New-Generation African Poets:
A Chapbook Box Set (Nane)
Edited by Kwame Dawes
and Chris Abani
(Akashic Books)

To order or obtain more information on these or other University of
Nebraska Press titles, visit nebraskapress.unl.edu. For more information
about the African Poetry Book Series, visit africanpoetrybf.unl.edu.